Everyday Life

There's Been a Death *Emily Dickinson* 56

London *William Blake* 58

The Schoolboy *William Blake* 60

Neighbours *Benjamin Zephaniah* 57

Street Boy *Gareth Owen* 59

Half-Term *U A Fanthorpe* 61

Emotion Recollected in Tranquillity

Windy Nights *Robert Louis Stevenson* 62

The Little Black Boy *William Blake* 64

Robert Bruce's March to Bannockburn *Robert Burns* 66

If *Rudyard Kipling* 68

A Tall Story *John Mole* 63

White Comedy *Benjamin Zephaniah* 65

Field of Vision *Seamus Heaney* 67

The Boy Who Danced With a Tank *Adrian Mitchell* 69

War

The Feast Of Crispian *William Shakespeare* 70

Lament for Culloden *Robert Burns* 72

Miners *Wilfred Owen* 74

The Drum *John Scott of Amwell* 76

Vergissmeinnicht *Keith Douglas* 71

Anne Frank Huis *Andrew Motion* 73

Lady in Black *Alun Lewis* 75

The Terror Years *Rajko Djurić* 77

God Moves in Mysterious Ways

Abou Ben Adhem *James Leigh Hunt* 78

Peace *Henry Vaughan* 80

Sundays *John Lyons* 79

Pax *D H Lawrence* 81

It's Only a Game

Vitaï Lampada *Henry Newbolt* 82

By the Waters of Liverpool *Adrian Mitchell* 83

The Open Road

The Pedlar's Caravan *William Brighty Rands* 84

The Long Road *Šaban Iliaz* 85

Time Past, Time Present

To the Virgins, to Make Much of Time *Robert Herrick* 86

The Poplar-Field *William Cowper* 88

Remember *Christina Rossetti* 90

Spring-Cleaning at Seventy *Edward Lowbury* 87

My Box *Gillian Clarke* 89

Fingers *Ted Hughes* 91

The Nativity Chant

Sir Walter Scott (1771-1832)

Canny moment, lucky fit;
Is the lady lighter yet?
Be it lad, or be it lass,
Sign wi' cross, and sain wi' mass.

Trefoil, vervain, John's-wort, dill,
Hinders witches of their will;
Weel is them, that weel may
Fast upon Saint Andrew's day.

Saint Bride and her brat,
Saint Colme and her cat,
Saint Michael and his spear,
Keep the house frae reif and wear.

Birth

POEMS

Th ow

Poetry Waters

EVANS BROTHERS LIMITED

Contents

Life cycle

The Nativity Chant Sir Walter Scott 6

Measles in the Ark Susan Coolidge 8

My Mistress' Eyes William Shakespeare 10

The Passionate Shepherd to His Love Christopher Marlowe 12

The Wedding Morning Thomas Hardy 14

On His Blindness John Milton 16

Steal Away to Jesus Spiritual 18

In Time of Pestilence Thomas Nashe 20

Death be not Proud John Donne 22

Crossing the Bar Alfred, Lord Tennyson 24

Morning Song Sylvia Plath 7

To My Mother George Barker 9

One Perfect Rose Dorothy Parker 11

When You Are Old WB Yeats 13

A Visit From My Mother-in-Law Judith Viorst 15

Second Opinion Douglas Dunn 17

Best Bone Paul Hyland 19

Twelve Songs IX WH Auden 21

Scattering the Ashes Andrew Fusek Peters 22

A Call Seamus Heaney 25

Visions

Dream-Pedlary Thomas Lovell Beddoes 26

La Belle Dame Sans Merci John Keats 28

He Wishes for the Cloths of Heaven WB Yeats 27

Fairy Story Stevie Smith 31

Natural World

The Windhover Gerard Manley Hopkins 32

By the Sea Christina Rossetti 34

Daffodils William Wordsworth 36

No! Thomas Hood 38

To Autumn John Keats 40

Address to a Child During a Boisterous
    Winter Evening Dorothy Wordsworth 42

The Tyger William Blake 46

Hares at Play John Clare 48

Widgeon Saumus Heaney 33

Waves Jackie Kay 35

Chickweed Edward Lowbury 37

Winter Andrew Young 39

Spring is Like a Perhaps Hand EE Cummings 41

Conspiracy of the Clouds Zulfikar Ghose 44

Moggy in the City Gareth Owen 47

Mooses Ted Hughes 49

Sounds

A Little Learning Alexander Pope 50

On First Looking Into Chapman's Homer John Keats 52

The Perils of Reading Fiction Adrian Mitchell 51

The Twenty-Sixers Philip Gross 54

MORNING SONG

Sylvia Plath (1932-1963)

Love set you going like a fat gold watch.
The midwife slapped your footsoles, and your bald cry
Took its place among the elements.

Our voices echo, magnifying your arrival.   New statue.
In a drafty museum, your nakedness
Shadows our safety. We stand round blankly as walls.

I'm no more your mother
Than the cloud that distils a mirror to reflect its own slow
Effacement at the wind's hand.

All night your moth-breath
Flickers among the flat pink roses. I wake to listen:
A far sea moves in my ear.

One cry, and I stumble from bed, cow-heavy and floral
In my Victorian nightgown.
Your mouth opens clean as a cat's. The window square

Whitens and swallows its dull stars. And now you try
Your handful of notes;
The clear vowels rise like balloons.

Measles in the Ark

Susan Coolidge (1835-1905)

The night it was horribly dark,
The measles broke out in the Ark;
Little Japheth, and Shem, and all the young Hams,
Were screaming at once for potatoes and clams.
And 'What shall I do,' said poor Mrs. Noah,
'All alone by myself in this terrible shower?
I know what I'll do: I'll step down in the hold,
And wake up a lioness grim and old,
And tie her close to the children's door,
And give her a ginger-cake to roar
At the top of her voice for an hour or more;
And I'll tell the children to cease their din,
Or I'll let that grim old party in,
To stop their squeazles and likewise their measles.'
She practised this with the greatest success:
She was everyone's grandmother, I guess.

TO MY MOTHER

George Barker (1913-)

Most near, most dear, most loved and most far,
Under the window where I often found her
Sitting as huge as Asia, seismic with laughter,
Gin and chicken helpless in her Irish hand,
Irresistible as Rabelais, but most tender for
The lame dogs and hurt birds that surround her, -
She is a procession no one can follow after
But be like a little dog following a brass band.

She will not glance up at the bomber, or condescend
To drop her gin and scuttle to a cellar,
But lean on the mahogany table like a mountain
Whom only faith can move, and so I send
O all my faith and all my love to tell her
That she will move from mourning into morning.

My Mistress' Eyes

William Shakespeare (1564-1616)

My mistress' eyes are nothing like the sun;
Coral is far more red than her lips' red;
If snow be white, why then her breasts are dun;
If hairs be wires, black wires grow on her head.
I have seen roses damasked, red and white,
But no such roses see I in her cheeks;
And in some perfumes is there more delight
Than in the breath that from my mistress reeks.
I love to hear her speak, yet well I know
That music hath a far more pleasing sound;
I grant I never saw a goddess go;
My mistress, when she walks, treads on the ground.
    And yet, by heaven, I think my love as rare
    As any she belied with false compare.

ONE PERFECT ROSE

Dorothy Parker (1893-1967)

A single flow'r he sent me, since we met.
   All tenderly his messenger he chose;
Deep-hearted, pure, with scented dew still wet -
   One perfect rose.

I knew the language of the floweret;
   'My fragile leaves,' it said, 'his heart enclose.'
Love long has taken for his amulet
   One perfect rose.

Why is it no one ever sent me yet
   One perfect limousine, do you suppose?
Ah no, it's always just my luck to get
   One perfect rose.

The Passionate Shepherd to His Love

Christopher Marlowe (1564-1593)

Come live with me and be my love,
And we will all the pleasures prove,
That hills and valleys, dales and fields,
And all the craggy mountains yields.

There we will sit upon the rocks,
And see the shepherds feed their flocks,
By shallow rivers to whose falls
Melodious birds sing madrigals.

And I will make thee beds of roses
With a thousand fragrant posies,
A cap of flowers, and a kirtle
Embroidered all with leaves of myrtle;

A gown made of the finest wool
Which from our pretty lambs we pull;
Fair linèd slippers for the cold,
With buckles of the purest gold;

A belt of straw and ivy buds,
With coral clasps and amber studs:
And if these pleasures may thee move,
Come live with me and be my love.

The shepherds' swains shall dance and sing
For thy delight each May morning:
If these delights thy mind may move,
Then live with me and be my love.

WHEN YOU ARE OLD

W B Yeats (1865-1939)

When you are old and grey and full of sleep,
And nodding by the fire, take down this book,
And slowly read, and dream of the soft look
Your eyes had once, and of their shadows deep;

How many loved your moments of glad grace,
And loved your beauty with love false or true,
But one man loved the pilgrim soul in you,
And loved the sorrows of your changing face;

And bending down beside the glowing bars,
Murmur, a little sadly, how Love fled
And paced upon the mountains overhead
And hid his face amid a crowd of stars.

Love

The Wedding Morning

Thomas Hardy (1840-1928)

Tabitha dressed for her wedding: -
'Tabby, why look so sad?'
' - O I feel a great gloominess spreading, spreading,
Instead of supremely glad! . . .

'I called on Carry last night,
And he came whilst I was there,
Not knowing I'd called. So I kept out of sight,
And I heard what he said to her:

" - Ah, I'd far liefer marry
You, Dear, to-morrow!" he said,
"But that cannot be." - O I'd give him to Carry,
And willingly see them wed,

'But how can I do it when
His baby will soon be born?
After that I hope I may die. And then
She can have him. I shall not mourn!'

Marriage

A VISIT FROM MY MOTHER-IN-LAW

Judith Viorst (c1930-)

My mother-in-law
Comes to visit
With her own apron
Her own jar of Nescafé
And the latest news.

Uncle Leo,
She's sorry to say,
Is divorcing Aunt Pearl.
Whose sister Bernice
Is having
A nervous breakdown.
The week
That they spent in Miami
It rained every day,
And her health,
Though she isn't complaining,
Has never been worse.
The lady upstairs
With the limp
Was attacked in broad daylight,
And Seymour her nephew
Has cataracts, flu,
And no job.

My husband,
She thinks she should mention,
Looks thin as a rail,
And the children,
It hurts her to hear,
Are coughing again,
Belle's son,
Only forty years old,
Dropped dead Friday morning,
And don't even bother
To ask
About cousin Rose.

I don't think I will.

On His Blindness

John Milton (1608-1674)

When I consider how my light is spent,
Ere half my days, in this dark world and wide,
And that one talent which is death to hide
Lodged with me useless, though my soul more bent
To serve therewith my Maker, and present
My true account, lest he returning chide,
'Doth God exact day-labour, light denied?'
I fondly ask. But Patience, to prevent
That murmur, soon replies:'God doth not need
Either man's work or his own gifts; who best
Bear his mild yoke, they serve him best. His state
Is kingly: thousands at his bidding speed,
And post o'er land and ocean without rest;
They also serve who only stand and wait.'

SECOND OPINION

Douglas Dunn (1942-)

We went to Leeds for a second opinion.
After her name was called,
I waited among the apparently well
And those with bandaged eyes and dark spectacles.

A heavy mother shuffled with bad feet
And a stick, a pad over one eye,
Leaving her children warned in their seats.
The minutes went by like a winter.

They called me in. What moment worse
Than that young doctor trying to explain?
'It's large and growing.' 'What is?' 'Malignancy.'
'Why *there*? She's an artist!'

He shrugged and said, 'Nobody knows.'
He warned me it might spread. 'Spread?'
My body ached to suffer like her twin
And touch the cure with lips and healing sesames.

No image, no straw to support me - nothing
To hear or see. No leaves rustling in sunlight.
Only the mind sliding against events
And the antiseptic whiff of destiny.

Professional anxiety -
His hand on my shoulder
Showing me to the door, a scent of soap,
Medical fingers, and his wedding ring.

Steal Away to Jesus

Spiritual

Steal away, steal away, steal away to Jesus,
Steal away, steal away home,
I ain't got long to stay here.

My Lord, He calls me,
He calls me by the thunder,
The trumpet sounds within-a my soul,
I ain't got long to stay here.

Steal away, steal away, steal away to Jesus,
Steal away, steal away home,
I ain't got long to stay here.

Green trees a-bending,
Po' sinner stands a-trembling,
The trumpet sounds within-a my soul,
I ain't got long to stay here.

Steal away, steal away, steal away to Jesus,
Steal away, steal away home,
I ain't got long to stay here.

old age

BEST BONE

Paul Hyland (1947-)

'I haven't often brewed up tea for two
since he passed on,' she smiles. I'm an imposter
posing here; a thief, that I shall have to
take myself away. 'My friends have gone,
I wonder why I stay to plague the young

like you, it was good of you to come.'
Her eye is fragile and her voice is thin.
The pottery is stout, a gay design
absurdly garish in her dim front room,
'It brightens up my mausoleum.'

She smiles again. I'd have expected
pastel porcelain that had survived
her years, perhaps her mother's. Instead
we drink from this. The fine stuff is displayed
behind glass in the corner cupboard.

The teacups there, some whole, some chipped or crazed,
gather no dust, that once were filled and raised
from this same lace to smiling lips of friends
whose grins now widen as the flesh recedes.
'What remains I want preserved.' She reads

the makes from memory, 'Best bone, but their
fragility and mine don't go together,
my sight is bad, I'm clumsy. I remember
mother beat me when I chipped her china.'
Her frail jaw juggles with soft laughter,

her knuckles whiten as she lifts the cup's
thick rim, so gently, to her parched blue lips,
steam clouds her eyes, and gently, as she sips,
age beats the living daylights out of her.

19

In Time of Pestilence

Thomas Nashe (1567-1601)

Adieu, farewell earth's bliss,
This world uncertain is;
Fond are life's lustful joys,
Death proves them all but toys,
None from his darts can fly.
I am sick, I must die.
       Lord, have mercy on us!

Rich men, trust not in wealth,
Gold cannot buy you health;
Physic himself must fade,
All things to end are made.
The plague full swift goes by.
I am sick, I must die.
       Lord, have mercy on us!

Beauty is but a flower
Which wrinkles will devour;
Brightness falls from the air,
Queens have died young and fair,
Dust hath closed Helen's eye.
I am sick, I must die.
       Lord, have mercy on us!

Strength stoops unto the grave,
Worms feed on Hector brave,
Swords may not fight with fate,
Earth still holds ope her gate.
Come! come! the bells do cry.
I am sick, I must die.
       Lord, have mercy on us!

Wit with his wantonness
Tasteth death's bitterness;
Hell's executioner
Hath no ears for to hear
What vain art can reply.
I am sick, I must die.
       Lord, have mercy on us!

Haste, therefore, each degree,
To welcome destiny.
Heaven is our heritage,
Earth but a player's stage;
Mount we unto the sky.
I am sick, I must die.
       Lord, have mercy on us!

TWELVE SONGS IX

W H Auden (1907-1973)

Stop all the clocks, cut off the telephone,
Prevent the dog from barking with a juicy bone,
Silence the pianos and with muffled drum
Bring out the coffin, let the mourners come.

Let aeroplanes circle moaning overhead
Scribbling on the sky the message He Is Dead,
Put crêpe bows round the white necks of the public doves,
Let the traffic policemen wear black cotton gloves.

He was my North, my South, my East and West,
My working week and my Sunday rest,
My noon, my midnight, my talk, my song;
I thought that love would last for ever: I was wrong.

The stars are not wanted now: put out every one;
Pack up the moon and dismantle the sun;
Pour away the ocean and sweep up the wood;
For nothing now can ever come to any good.

Death be not proud

John Donne (1572-1631)

Death, be not proud, though some have called thee
Mighty and dreadful, for thou are not so:
For those whom thou think'est thou dost overthrow
Die not, poor Death, nor yet canst thou kill me.
From rest and sleep, which but thy pictures be,
Much pleasure; then from thee much more must flow,
And soonest our best men with thee do go,
Rest of their bones, and soul's delivery.
Thou'art slave to fate, chance, kings, and desperate men,
And dost with poison, war, and sickness dwell,
And poppy'or charms can make us sleep as well
And better than thy stroke; why swell'st thou then?
One short sleep past, we wake eternally,.
And death shall be no more; Death, thou shalt die.

SCATTERING THE ASHES
Andrew Fusek Peters (1965-)

Ah! you have gone and all that is left is words
that ring like dull bells on my tongue
and my mouth is dry
as the ashes of your body.
For one whole year
and a month,
we held you in a plastic bag,
airtight - for there was no longer any need to breathe.
And you sat in the living room of our mother's house,
squat, monolithic in your black-cornered container.

Easy to say the spirit had gone,
jumping out from your body as the last breath exhaled.
Yet in those clustered granules
were hands I held,
rough scraping chin,
your gangly angularities,
the dark eyes I begin to forget.

And so we took you, my brother,
up onto the hill,
with scissors and bags and hands,
ready to dip into you,
the bitterest sherbet.

We found an avenue of trees,
a lane of childish days
where women with dogs avoided us,
the weeping mother,
the cold-eyed son
unable to comprehend the vastness of his grief.
We scooped you up
to place you at the beginning of each trunk,
an offering, a grey sacrifice,
and for a second,
as my hands grew powdered
I wondered with horror
if that which killed you,
lived still in this sickened chalk.

22

And my mother, laden with the years,
the endless avenue of deaths which she had had to walk,
fell to the grass and cried out
at this ancient and greek tragedy,
on the hill that myth said was made by bodies from the plague.

We stumbled home to finish the job
of spreading my brother out
in the places we best remembered,
and in the garden
I gathered my handfuls
and sowed at last my tears,
One for the wasp's nest,
One for the pear tree,
One for the feast,
One for the fire,
One for the den, and
One for the cut down willow,
where we played the perfect game of hide and seek.

You are hidden now,
cut down in the maleness of your days.
We have buried the last of you
by the roots of a young and eager silver birch.
My mother is made grey by your ashes
and your terrible gift to me
is an oldness in my youth
and a fear of death
that cannot see the life growing inside my wife's womb.
This is a dark day,
I would, if I could now put it away,
to scatter its shadows
among the many-memoried summers we shared.

Crossing the Bar

Alfred, Lord Tennyson (1809-1892)

Sunset and evening star,
   And one clear call for me!
And may there be no moaning of the bar,
   When I put out to sea,

But such a tide as moving seems asleep,
   Too full for sound and foam,
When that which drew from out the boundless deep
   Turns again home.

Twilight and evening bell,
   And after that the dark!
And may there be no sadness of farewell,
   When I embark;

For though from out our bourne of Time and Place
   The flood may bear me far,
I hope to see my Pilot face to face
   When I have crost the bar.

Death

A CALL

Seamus Heaney (1939-)

'Hold on,' she said, 'I'll just run out and get him.
The weather here's so good, he took the chance
To do a bit of weeding.'
             So I saw him
Down on his hands and knees beside the leek rig,
Touching, inspecting, separating one
Stalk from the other, gently pulling up
Everything not tapered, frail and leafless,
Pleased to feel each little weed-root break,
But rueful also …
             Then found myself listening to
The amplified grave ticking of hall clocks
Where the phone lay unattended in a calm
Of mirror glass and sunstruck pendulums…

And found myself then thinking: if it were nowadays,
This is how Death would summon Everyman.

Next thing he spoke and I nearly said I loved him.

Dream-Pedlary

Thomas Lovell Beddoes (1803-1849)

If there were dreams to sell
   What would you buy?
Some cost a passing bell,
   Some a light sigh,
That shakes from Life's fresh crown
Only a rose-leaf down.
If there were dreams to sell,
Merry and sad to tell,
And the crier rang the bell,
   What would you buy?

A cottage lone and still,
   With bowers nigh,
Shadowy, my woes to still
   Until I die.
Such pearl from Life's fresh crown
Fain would I shake me down.
Were dreams to have at will,
This would best heal my ill,
   This would I buy.

But there were dreams to sell,
   Ill didst thou buy;
Life is a dream, they tell,
   Waking, to die.
Dreaming a dream to prize,
Is wishing ghosts to rise;
   And, if I had the spell
   To call the buried, well,
   Which one would I?

If there are ghosts to raise,
   What shall I call,
Out of hell's murky haze,
   Heaven's blue hall?
Raise my loved long-lost boy
To lead me to his joy.
   There are no ghosts to raise;
   Out of death lead no ways;
   Vain is the call.

Know'st thou not ghosts to sue?
   No love thou hast.
Else lie, as I will do,
   And breathe thy last.
So out of Life's fresh crown
Fall like a rose-leaf down.
   Thus are the ghosts to woo;
   Thus are all dreams made true,
   Ever to last!

Dreams

HE WISHES FOR THE CLOTHS OF HEAVEN

W B Yeats (1865-1939)

Had I the heavens' embroidered cloths,
Enwrought with golden and silver light,
The blue and the dim and the dark cloths
Of night and light and the half-light,
I would spread the cloths under your feet:
But I, being poor, have only my dreams;
I have spread my dreams under your feet;
Tread softly because you tread on my dreams.

La Belle Dame Sans Merci

John Keats (1795-1821)

'O what can ail thee, knight-at-arms,
    Alone and palely loitering?
The sedge has withered from the lake,
    And no birds sing.

'O what can ail thee, knight-at-arms,
    So haggard and so woe-begone?
The squirrel's granary is full,
    And the harvest's done.

'I see a lily on thy brow
    With anguish moist and fever dew;
And on thy cheek a fading rose
    Fast withereth too.'

'I met a lady in the meads,
    Full beautiful - a faery's child,
Her hair was long, her foot was light,
    And her eyes were wild.

'I made a garland for her head,
    And bracelets too, and fragrant zone;
She looked at me as she did love,
    And made sweet moan.

'I set her on my pacing steed
    And nothing else saw all day long,
For sideways would she lean, and sing
    A faery's song.

Fairy Stories

'She found me roots of relish sweet,
  And honey wild and manna dew,
And sure in language strange she said,
   "I love thee true!"

'She took me to her elfin grot,
  And there she wept and sighed full sore;
And there I shut her wild, wild eyes
   With kisses four.

'And there she lullèd me asleep,
  And there I dreamed - Ah! woe betide!
The latest dream I ever dreamed
   On the cold hill's side.

'I saw pale kings and princes too,
  Pale warriors, death-pale were they all;
Who cried - "La belle Dame sans Merci
   Hath thee in thrall!"

'I saw their starved lips in the gloam
  With horrid warning gapèd wide,
And I awoke and found me here
   On the cold hill's side.

'And this is why I sojourn here
  Alone and palely loitering,
Though the sedge is withered from the lake,
   And no birds sing.'

FAIRY STORY

Stevie Smith (1902-1971)

I went into the wood one day
And there I walked and lost my way

When it was so dark I could not see
A little creature came to me

He said if I would sing a song
The time would not be very long

But first I must let him hold my hand tight
Or else the wood would give me a fright

I sang a song, he let me go
But now I am home again there is nobody I know.

The Windhover

To Christ Our Lord

Gerard Manley Hopkins (1844-1889)

I caught this morning morning's minion, king-
dom of daylight's dauphin, dapple-dawn-drawn Falcon,
in his riding.
   Of the rolling level underneath him steady air, and striding
High there, how he rung upon the rein of a wimpling wing
In his ecstasy! then off, off forth on swing,
   As a skate's heel sweeps smooth on a bow-bend: the hurl and
     gliding
   Rebuffed the big wind. My heart in hiding
Stirred for a bird, - the achieve of, the mastery of the thing!

Brute beauty and valour and act, oh, air, pride, plume, here
   Buckle! AND the fire that breaks from thee then, a billion
Times told lovelier, more dangerous, O my chevalier!

   No wonder of it: sheer plod makes plough down sillion
Shine, and blue-bleak embers, ah my dear,
   Fall, gall themselves, and gash gold-vermilion.

Birdsong

WIDGEON

Seamus Heaney (1939-)   for Paul Muldoon

It had been badly shot.
While he was plucking it
he found, he says, the voice box -

like a flute stop
in the broken windpipe -

and blew upon it
unexpectedly
his own small widgeon cries.

By the Sea

Christina Rossetti (1830-1894)

Why does the sea moan evermore?
Shut out from heaven it makes its moan,
It frets against the boundary shore:
All earth's full rivers cannot fill
The sea, that drinking thirsteth still.

Sheer miracles of loveliness
Lie hid in its unlooked-on bed:
Anemones, salt, passionless,
Blow flower-like - just enough alive
To blow and multiply and thrive.

Shells quaint with curve or spot or spike,
Encrusted live things argus-eyed,
All fair alike yet all unlike,
Are born without a pang, and die
Without a pang, and so pass by.

WAVES

Jackie Kay (1961-)

There are waves to chase and waves that crash,
There are waves to jump like skipping ropes,
Waves to run away to sand, waves to leap and bound.
Waves that are turquoise, waves that are brown,
Waves full of seaweed, waves that drown.
Waves clear and calm, waves angry and wronged,
Waves that whisper, waves that roar like thunder,
Waves you'd never swim under, pounding rocks and shore.

Waves that put you to sleep, sssh sssh sssh cradle-rock.
Waves that look like sea horses or sheep or curly froth.
Waves that are cold as bare floor, waves that are warm as toast.
There are waves called the Black Sea, the Red Sea, the North Sea,
Waves called the Pacific ocean, the Atlantic ocean, the Antarctic.
If you counted them all, wave upon wave upon wave
would it be a hundred, a thousand, a billion - or more?

Daffodils

William Wordsworth (1770-1850)

I wandered lonely as a cloud
That floats on high o'er vales and hills,
When all at once I saw a crowd,
A host, of golden daffodils;
Beside the lake, beneath the trees,
Fluttering and dancing in the breeze.

Continuous as the stars that shine
And twinkle on the Milky Way,
They stretched in never-ending line
Along the margin of a bay:
Ten thousand saw I at a glance,
Tossing their heads in sprightly dance.

The waves beside them danced, but they
Out-did the sparkling waves in glee:
A poet could not but be gay,
In such a jocund company:
I gazed - and gazed - but little thought
What wealth the show to me had brought.

For oft, when on my couch I lie
In vacant or in pensive mood,
They flash upon that inward eye
Which is the bliss of solitude;
And then my heart with pleasure fills,
And dances with the daffodils.

CHICKWEED

Edward Lowbury (1913-)

Definitive weed, but starriest of flowers,
   I pluck huge armfuls of you from the rosebed,
    Then mutter apologies: I'm half ashamed
Of having scotched your blaze of tiny stars,
Cut short a living galaxy. My peace
    Of mind is oddly jarred; soothing my nerves,
    I say that I have killed the weeds to save
The roses. Now I'm trying to save face …
Soon they will hatch, dog roses, floribunda;
    No doubt I'll sing their praise, as I have done
    Each summer, but this year I will reserve
Some harmony, some living words of wonder
For midget, self-effacing stars of day
Which live, outshining midnight's Milky Way.

Flowers

NO!

Thomas Hood (1799-1845)

No sun - no moon!
No morn - no noon -
No dawn - no dusk - no proper time of day -
No sky - no earthly view -
No distance looking blue -
No road - no street - no 't'other side the way' -
No end to any Row -
No indications where the Crescents go -
No top to any steeple -
No recognitions of familiar people -
No courtesies for showing 'em -
No knowing 'em! -
No travelling at all - no locomotion,
No inkling of the way - no notion -
'No go' - by land or ocean -
No mail - no post -
No news from any foreign coast -
No Park - no Ring - no afternoon gentility -
No company - no nobility -
No warmth, no cheerfulness, no healthful ease,
No comfortable feel in any member -
No shade, no shine, no butterflies, no bees,
No fruits, no flowers, no leaves, no birds -
November!

Winter

WINTER

Andrew Young (1885-1971)

Time, like an aged gardener,
Still tends the garden of the year,
And, when the summer sweets are lost,
He weaves the scentless flowers of frost.

When, too, the forest boughs have shed
Their generation of the dead,
Against the stars the sacred trees
Spread out their naked traceries.

And in the night an amorous moon
Sings to the sea a tender tune,
And all the star-encrusted sky
Shivers with silent ecstacy.

For Beauty thus not only glows
Within the wine-cup of the rose,
But like a hermit clad may be
In garment of austerity.

To Autumn

John Keats (1795-1821)

Season of mists and mellow fruitfulness!
    Close bosom-friend of the maturing sun;
Conspiring with him how to load and bless
    With fruit the vines that round the thatch-eaves run;
To bend with apples the mossed cottage-trees,
    And fill all fruit with ripeness to the core;
        To swell the gourd, and plump the hazel shells
With a sweet kernel; to set budding more,
    And still more, later flowers for the bees,
    Until they think warm days will never cease,
        For Summer has o'erbrimmed their clammy cells.

Who hath not seen thee oft amid thy store?
    Sometimes whoever seeks abroad may find
Thee sitting careless on a granary floor,
    Thy hair soft-lifted by the winnowing wind,
Or on a half-reaped furrow sound asleep,
    Drowsed with the fume of poppies, while thy hook
        Spares the next swath and all its twinèd flowers;
And sometimes like a gleaner thou dost keep
    Steady thy laden head across a brook;
    Or by a cider-press, with patient look,
        Thou watchest the last oozings hours by hours.

The turning year

Where are the songs of Spring? Ay, where are they?
Think not of them, thou hast thy music too, -
While barred clouds bloom the soft-dying day,
And touch the stubble-plains with rosy hue;
Then in a wailful choir the small gnats mourn
Among the river sallows, borne aloft
Or sinking as the light wind lives or dies;
And full-grown lambs loud bleat from hilly bourn;
Hedge-crickets sing; and now with treble soft
The redbreast whistles from a garden-croft;
And gathering swallows twitter in the skies.

SPRING IS LIKE A PERHAPS HAND

EE Cummings (1894-1962)

Spring is like a perhaps hand
(which comes carefully
out of Nowhere)arranging
a window, into which people look(while
people stare
arranging and changing placing
carefully there a strange
thing and a known thing here)and

changing everything carefully

spring is like a perhaps
Hand in a window
(carefully to
and fro moving New and
Old things,while
people stare carefully
moving a perhaps
fraction of flower here placing
an inch of air there)and

without breaking anything.

Address to a Child During a Boisterous Winter Evening

Dorothy Wordsworth (1771-1855)

What way does the Wind come? What way does he go?
He rides over the water, and over the snow,
Through wood, and through vale; and o'er rocky height,
Which the goat cannot climb, takes his sounding flight;
He tosses about in every bare tree,
As, if you look up, you plainly may see;
But how he will come, and whither he goes,
There's never a scholar in England knows.

He will suddenly stop in a cunning nook,
And rings a sharp 'larum; but, if you should look,
There's nothing to see but a cushion of snow
Round as a pillow, and whiter than milk,
And softer than if it were covered with silk.
Sometimes he'll hide in the cave of a rock,
Then whistle as shrill as the buzzard cock.
Yet seek him - and what shall you find in his place?
Nothing but silence and empty space;
Save, in a corner, a heap of dry leaves,
That he's left, for a bed, to beggars or thieves!

As soon as 'tis daylight, tomorrow with me
You shall go to the orchard, and then you will see
That he has been there, and made a great rout,
And cracked the branches, and strewn them about:
Heaven grant that he spare but that one upright twig
That looked up at the sky so proud and big
All last summer, as well you know,
Studded with apples, a beautiful show!

Hark! over the roof he makes a pause,
And growls as if he would fix his claws
Right in the slates, and with a huge rattle
Drive them down, like men in a battle.
But let him range round; he does us no harm,
We build up the fire, we're snug and warm;
Untouched by his breath, see the candle shines bright,
And burns with a clear and steady light.
Books have we to read - but that half-stifled knell,
Alas! 'tis the sound of the eight o'clock bell.

Come, now we'll to bed! and when we are there
He may work his own will, and what shall we care?
He may knock at the door - we'll not let him in;
May drive at the windows - we'll laugh at his din.
Let him seek his own home, wherever it be:
Here's a cosy warm house for Edward and me.

CONSPIRACY OF THE CLOUDS

Zulfikar Ghose (1935-)

In the afternoon the clouds became transparent.

The satellite pictures and the computer data
had indicated a tropical depression
in the Gulf. The weathermen flew out
expecting to enter the eye of the hurricane
as it formed on the coast of Louisiana
but found themselves flying in a blue sky
with not even clear-air turbulence
to record on their sensitive machines.

What had happened to the atmosphere?

The jet stream entering the continent
in northern California and dropping down
across New Mexico and Texas before
flowing over Maryland ought to have been
creating an upper-air disturbance. With
a dense flow of humid air from the Yucatan
pushing all the way to North Dakota,
the conditions were right for tornadoes.

But still the whole of the U.S. was without a cloud.

Suddenly the meteorologists got excited seeing
confirmed reports of low pressure across Kansas;
the potential was building right in the heart
of the country for really violent weather.

But now the satellite pictures picked up nothing!

Nothing but blue sky everywhere.
Even the astronauts on the space shuttle
looked down on a cloudless America.

The next day heavy rain fell and took
the farmers of Nebraska by surprise -
it had certainly not been forecast; what's more,
there wasn't a cloud visible in the sky.
The question everyone asked: Where is this
rain coming from, why weren't we told about it?

The Tyger

William Blake (1757-1827)

Tyger! Tyger! burning bright
In the forests of the night,
What immortal hand or eye
Could frame thy fearful symmetry?

In what distant deeps or skies
Burnt the fire of thine eyes?
On what wings dare he aspire?
What the hand dare seize the fire?

And what shoulder, and what art,
Could twist the sinews of thy heart?
And when thy heart begin to beat,
What dread hand? And what dread feet?

What the hammer? what the chain?
In what furnace was thy brain?
What the anvil? what dread grasp
Dare its deadly terrors clasp?

When the stars threw down their spears,
And water'd heaven with their tears,
Did he smile his work to see?
Did he who made the Lamb make thee?

Tyger! Tyger! Burning bright
In the forests of the night,
What immortal hand or eye
Dare frame thy fearful symmetry?

MOGGY IN THE CITY

Gareth Owen (1936-)

Old fat moggy
Padding on grimy cobbles
Slouching past washing
Rooting in dustbins
Picking your way past puddles
Gliding down ginnels
Miaowling on walls
Purring and rubbing
Round mothers and prams
Rambling through rubbish heaps
Crouching in old cars
Treading the streets
Of dirty old Mother Liverpool.
You,
I feel,
Deserved more
But you betray no resentment
In slow-closing eyes
And somehow with stripes
And regal softness
Make our city better.

Cats big and small

Hares at Play

John Clare (1793-1864)

The birds are gone to bed, the cows are still,
And sheep lie panting on each old mole-hill;
And underneath the willow's grey-green bough,
Like toil a-resting, lies the fallow plough.
The timid hares throw daylight fears away
On the lane's road to dust and dance and play,
Then dabble in the grain by naught deterred
To lick the dew-fall from the barley's beard;
Then out they sturt again and round the hill
Like happy thoughts dance, squat, and loiter still,
Till milking maidens in the early morn
Jingle their yokes and sturt them in the corn;
Through well-known beaten paths each nimbling hare
Sturts quick as fear, and seeks its hidden lair.

Animals

MOOSES

Ted Hughes (1930-1999)

The goofy Moose, the walking house-frame,
Is lost
In the forest.   He bumps, he blunders, he stands.

With massy bony thoughts sticking out near his
    ears -
Reaching out palm upwards, to catch whatever
    might be falling from heaven -
He tries to think,
Leaning their huge weight
On the lectern of his front legs.

He can't find the world!
Where did it go? What does a world look like?
The Moose
Crashes on, and crashes into a lake, and stares at
    the mountain and cries:
'Where do I belong? This is no place!'

He turns dragging half the lake out after him
And charges the cackling underbrush -

He meets another Moose
He stares, he thinks: 'It's only a mirror!'
'Where is the world?' he groans. 'O my lost world!
And why am I so ugly?
And why am I so far away from my feet?'

He weeps.
Hopeless drops drip from his droopy lips.

The other Moose just stands there doing the same.

Two dopes of the deep woods.

A Little Learning

Alexander Pope (1688-1744)

A little learning is a dangerous thing;
Drink deep, or taste not the Pierian spring:
There shallow draughts intoxicate the brain,
And drinking largely sobers us again.
Fired at first sight with what the Muse imparts,
In fearless youth we tempt the heights of Arts;
While from the bounded level of our mind
Short views we take, nor see the lengths behind,
But, more advanced, behold with strange surprise
New distant scenes of endless science rise!
So pleased at first the towering Alps we try,
Mount o'er the vales, and seem to tread the sky;
The eternal snows appear already past,
And the first clouds and mountains seem the last:
But those attained, we tremble to survey
The growing labours of the lengthened way;
The increasing prospect tires our wandering eyes,
Hills peep o'er hills, and Alps on Alps arise!

Words

THE PERILS OF READING FICTION

Adrian Mitchell (1932-)

If you read too many books with made-up stories you go a bit mad
That's what my Sergeant used to say every time he saw anyone
      reading
All those writers, most of them foreign and dead,
With their freaky ideas and nancy ways and gone with the
      how'syourfather
All those Swish Family Robinsons and Lorna Dooms and King
      Falstaffs
And The Great Fatsby and Virginia Beowulf and Kubla Khan-Khan
And Jane Austen and Jane Morris and Jane Volkswagen
All of em jumbled up and tripping over each other in your brainbox
Well it's like letting a year's worth of dreams out of a corrall
To stampede all over your real life, all those pretty lies and ugly lies,
Whirling about inside your skull, beating up storms of yellow dust
So soon you can't see for the grit in the eyes, you can't look out at all
And see the real world which is just the real world
And is real and not made up by somebody trying to be clever -
Listen - what I say is -
If you read too many books with made-up stories you go a bit mad.

On First Looking Into Chapman's Homer

John Keats (1795-1821)

Much have I travelled in the realms of gold,
　　　And many goodly states and kingdoms seen;
　　　Round many western islands have I been
Which bards in fealty to Apollo hold.
Oft of one wide expanse had I been told
　　　That deep-browed Homer ruled as his demesne:
　　　Yet did I never breathe its pure serene
Till I heard Chapman speak out loud and bold:
Then felt I like some watcher of the skies
　　　When a new planet swims into his ken;
Or like stout Cortez, when with eagle eyes
　　　He stared at the Pacific - and all his men
Looked at each other with a wild surmise -
　　　Silent, upon a peak in Darien.

THE TWENTY-SIXERS

Philip Gross (1952-)

We are the twenty-sixers:
gypsies, jugglers, necromancers.
Hear, sir, here we come:
Fortune-tellers, cheapjack tricksters.
Cross our palm, sir. Join our dance, sir,
or we'll strike you dumb.

An Angel Arguing with an Ancient Ape …
A Bishop Breaking Bread with a Baboon …
A Carrion Crow Clad in a Crimson Cape …
A Doctor of Divinity who Dreams of Doom …

We are the twenty-sixers:
gypsies, jugglers, necromancers.
Hear, sir, here we come:
Fortune-tellers, cheapjack tricksters.
Cross our palm, sir. Join our dance, sir,
or we'll strike you dumb.

An Eccentric Earl with Eagles to Exhibit …
A Fund to Finance Fiends who Fail to Fall …
A Goblin Gabbling Grace beneath a Gibbet …
The Hounds of Hopelessness that Howl around the Hall …

An Intellectual Imp Inventing Interesting Ills …
A Jumped-up Judge who Jokes about the Jews …
The Kids in Khaki every Kind of Kingdom Kills …
Lieutenant Luck who Lends them Lives to Lose …

We are the twenty-sixers:
gypsies, jugglers, necromancers.
Hear, sir, here we come:
Fortune-tellers, cheapjack tricksters.
Cross our palm, sir. Join our dance, sir,
or we'll strike you dumb.

The Monstrous Maybes in the Mire of Might-Have-Been …
The Nevermores that Nag you in the Night …
The Odd One Out who's Only Out on Hallowe'en …
The Princess Pretty-Please who's Painfully Polite …

The Questionmark that can't Quite Quench your Quest …
The Ringing of a Right and Royal Rhyme …
The Silent Song that cannot be Suppressed …
The Ticks and Tocks that Take their Toll of Time …

We are the twenty-sixers:
gypsies, jugglers, necromancers.
Hear, sir, here we come:
Fortune-tellers, cheapjack tricksters.
Cross our palm, sir. Join our dance, sir,
or we'll strike you dumb.

The Undertaker's Ugly Understudy, Ulf …
The Violent Vicar whom his Victims' Vex …
The Woman Who Went Walking With a Wolf …
The letter the unlettered sign with: X

The Youth who Yawns but Yearns to Yell out *Yes!* …
The Zombie with his Zip stuck in the Zoo …
But without a twenty-seventh we are less
than breaths of wind. So we have come for you.

We are the twenty-sixers:
gypsies, jugglers, necromancers.
Hear, sir, here we come:
Fortune-tellers, cheapjack tricksters.
Cross our palm, sir. Join our dance, sir,
or we'll strike you dumb.

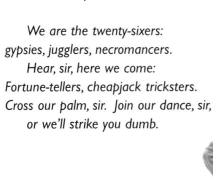

There's Been a Death

Emily Dickinson (1830-1886)

There's been a Death, in the Opposite House,
As lately as Today -
I know it, by the numb look
Such Houses have - alway -

The Neighbours rustle in and out -
The Doctor - drives away -
A Window opens like a Pod -
Abrupt - mechanically -

Somebody flings A mattress out -
The Children hurry by -
They wonder if it died - on that -
I used to - when a Boy -

The Minister - goes stiffly in -
As if the House were His -
And He owned all the Mourners - now -
And little Boys - besides -

And then the Milliner - and the Man
Of the Appalling Trade -
To take the measure of the House -

There'll be that Dark Parade -

Of Tassels - and of Coaches - soon -
It's easy as a Sign -
The Intuition of the News -
In just a Country Town.

NEIGHBOURS

Benjamin Zephaniah (1958-)

I am the type you are supposed to fear
Black and foreign
Big and dreadlocks
An uneducated grass eater.

I talk in tongues
I chant at night
I appear anywhere,
I sleep with lions
And when the moon gets me
I am a Wailer.

I am moving in
Next door to you
So you can get to know me,
You will see my shadow
In the bathroom window,
My aromas will occupy
Your space,
Our ball will be in your court.
How will you feel?

You should feel good
You have been chosen.

I am the type you are supposed to love
Dark and mysterious
Tall and natural
Thinking, tea total.
I talk in schools
I sing on TV
I am in the papers,
I keep cool cats

And when the sun is shining
I go Carnival.

London

William Blake (1757-1827)

I wander through each chartered street,
Near where the chartered Thames does flow,
And mark in every face I meet
Marks of weakness, marks of woe.

In every cry of every man,
In every infant's cry of fear,
In every voice, in every ban,
The mind-forged manacles I hear.

How the chimney-sweeper's cry
Every blackening church appalls;
And the hapless soldier's sigh
Runs in blood down palace walls.

But most through midnight streets I hear
How the youthful harlot's curse
Blasts the newborn infant's tear,
And blights with plagues the marriage hearse.

Citybeat

STREET BOY

Gareth Owen (1936-)

Just you look at me, man,
Stompin' down the street
My crombie stuffed with biceps
My boots is filled with feet.

Just you hark to me, man,
When they call us out
My head is full of silence
My mouth is full of shout.

Just you watch me move, man,
Steady like a clock
My heart is spaced on blue beat
My soul is stoned on rock.

Just you read my name, man,
Writ for all to see
The walls is red with stories
The streets is filled with me.

The Schoolboy

William Blake (1757-1827)

I love to rise in a summer morn
When the birds sing on every tree;
The distant huntsman winds his horn,
And the sky-lark sings with me.
O! what sweet company.

But to go to school in a summer morn,
O! it drives all joy away;
Under a cruel eye outworn,
The little ones spend the day
In sighing and dismay.

Ah! then at times I drooping sit,
And spend many an anxious hour,
Nor in my book can I take delight,
Nor sit in learning's bower,
Worn thro' with the dreary shower.

How can the bird that is born for joy
Sit in a cage and sing?
How can a child, when fears annoy,
But droop his tender wing,
And forget his youthful spring?

HALF-TERM

U.A.Fanthorpe (1929-)

Always autumn, in my memory.
Butter ringing the drilled teashop crumpets;
Handmade chocolates, rich enough to choke
    you,
Brought in special smooth paper from Town.

(Back at school, the square tall piles
Of bread, featureless red jam in basins,
Grace, a shuffle of chairs, the separate table
For the visiting lacrosse team.)

Long awkward afternoons in hotel lounges,
Islanded in swollen armchairs, eyeing
Aristocratic horses in irrelevant magazines.
Should I be talking to Them?

(Back at school the raptly selfish
Snatch at self: the clashing
Determined duets in cold practising-
Room, the passionate solitary knitting.)

Inadequacies of presentation, perceived
By parents' temporary friends; hair, manners,
Clothes, have failed to adjust.
I don't know the rules of snooker.

(Back at school, the stiff reliable
Awkwardness of work.   History test
On Monday morning.   Deponent verbs.
I have never been good at maths.)

Saying goodbye. There are tears
And hugs, relief, regret. They,
Like me, return to a patterned life
Whose rules are easy.   Unworthily

I shall miss chocolate, crumpets,
Comfort, but not the love I only
Sense as they go, waving to the end,
Vague in the streetlamps of November.

(Back at school the bullies,
Tyrants and lunatics are waiting.
I can deal with them.)

Windy Nights

Robert Louis Stevenson (1850-1894)

Whenever the moon and stars are set,
Whenever the wind is high,
All night long in the dark and wet,
A man goes riding by.
Late in the night when the fires are out,
Why does he gallop and gallop about?

Whenever the trees are crying aloud,
And ships are tossed at sea,
By, on the highway, low and loud,
By at the gallop goes he.
By at the gallop he goes, and then
By he comes back at the gallop again.

Imagination

A TALL STORY

John Mole   (1941-)

Yesterday Miss Williams told the class
'Use your imagination!
Everybody, close their eyes
(you too, Sophie).
Now what can you see?'

'Miss,' said Sophie, grinning,
'there's a baby alligator
lying on your desk.
He likes you, look,
his legs are waving in the air.
I think he wants his tummy tickled.'

'Well done, Sophie.
Excellent. Thank you.   Everybody
open your eyes now.'
So we did.

And there he was, the alligator,
just like Sophie said,
and when Miss Williams
had tickled him enough she popped him
head-down in her handbag
with his scaley, waving
tail-tip sticking out.

'See you later, pet,'
she said,
'but, children, that's enough of that.
Pick up your pencils, now,
it's time to write' . . .

At break-time, all of us
went up to Sophie
as she stood there, gobsmacked,
like a conjuror's assistant
who had managed her own trick.
'Sophie, you're brilliant,'
we told her.
'Wait till you hear *our* stories' . . .

Later, back home,
my Mum, as usual, asked me
what I'd done today at school
and (when I told her) just for once
she didn't say '*That Sophie!*' like she
always did but simply

'You and your imagination!'

The Little Black Boy

William Blake (1757-1827)

My mother bore me in the southern wild,
And I am black, but O! my soul is white;
White as an angel is the English child:
But I am black as if bereav'd of light.

My mother taught me underneath a tree,
And sitting down before the heat of day,
She took me on her lap and kiséd me,
And pointing to the east, began to say:

"Look on the rising sun: there God does live,
And gives his light, and gives his heat away;
And flowers and trees and beasts and men receive
Comfort in morning, joy in the noon day.

"And we are put on earth a little space,
That we may learn to bear the beams of love,
And these black bodies and this sun-burnt face
Is but a cloud, and like a shady grove.

"For when our souls have learn'd the heat to bear,
The cloud will vanish; we shall hear his voice,
Saying:'Come out from the grove, my love & care,
And round my golden tent like lambs rejoice.'"

Thus did my mother say, and kiséd me;
And thus I say to little English boy:
When I from black and he from white cloud free,
And round the tent of God like lambs we joy,

I'll shade him from the heat till he can bear
To lean in joy upon our father's knee;
And then I'll stand and stroke his silver hair,
And be like him, and he will then love me.

WHITE COMEDY

Benjamin Zephaniah (1958-)

I waz whitemailed
By a white witch,
Wid white magic
An white lies,
Branded a white sheep
I slaved as a whitesmith
Near a white spot
Where I suffered whitewater fever.
Whitelisted as a white leg
I waz in de white book
As a master of de white art,
It waz like white death.

People called me white jack
Some hailed me as white wog,
So I joined de white watch
Trained as a white guard
Lived off de white economy.
Caught an beaten by de whiteshirts
I waz condemned to a white mass.

Don't worry,
I shall be writing to de Black House.

Double negative

Robert Bruce's March to Bannockburn

Robert Burns (1759-1796)

Scots, wha hae wi' Wallace bled,
Scots, wham Bruce has aften led,
Welcome to your gory bed,
    Or to victory!

Now's the day, and now's the hour;
See the front o' battle lour,
See approach proud Edward's power -
    Chains and slavery!

Wha will be a traitor knave?
Wha can fill a coward's grave?
Wha sae base as be a slave? -
    Let him turn, and flee!

Wha for Scotland's King and Law
Freedom's sword will strongly draw,
Freeman stand or freeman fa',
    Let him follow me!

By Oppression's woes and pains,
By your sons in servile chains,
We will drain our dearest veins,
    But they shall be free!

Lay the proud usurpers low!
Tyrants fall in every foe!
Liberty's in every blow!
    Let us do, or die!

Courage

FIELD OF VISION

Seamus Heaney (1939-)

I remember this woman who sat for years
In a wheelchair, looking straight ahead
Out the window at sycamore trees unleafing
And leafing at the far end of the lane.

Straight out past the TV in the corner,
The stunted, agitated hawthorn bush,
The same small calves with their backs to wind and rain,
The same acre of ragwort, the same mountain.

She was steadfast as the big window itself.
Her brow was clear as the chrome bits of the chair.
She never lamented once and she never
Carried a spare ounce of emotional weight.

Face to face with her was an education
Of the sort you got across a well-braced gate -
One of those lean, clean, iron, roadside ones
Between two whitewashed pillars, where you could see

Deeper into the country than you expected
And discovered that the field behind the hedge
Grew more distinctly strange as you kept standing
Focused and drawn in by what barred the way.

If

Rudyard Kipling (1865-1936)

If you can keep your head when all about you
Are losing theirs and blaming it on you;
If you can trust yourself when all men doubt you,
But make allowance for their doubting too;
If you can wait and not be tired by waiting,
Or, being lied about, don't deal in lies,
Or, being hated, don't give way to hating,
And yet don't look too good, nor talk too wise;

If you can dream - and not make dreams your master;
If you can think - and not make thoughts your aim;
If you can meet with triumph and disaster
And treat those two impostors just the same;
If you can bear to hear the truth you've spoken
Twisted by knaves to make a trap for fools,
Or watch the things you gave your life to broken,
And stoop and build 'em up with wornout tools;

If you can make one heap of all your winnings
And risk it on one turn of pitch-and-toss,
And lose, and start again at your beginnings
And never breathe a word about your loss;
If you can force your heart and nerve and sinew
To serve your turn long after they are gone,
And so hold on when there is nothing in you
Except the Will which says to them: 'Hold on';

If you can talk with crowds and keep your virtue,
Or walk with kings - nor lose the common touch;
If neither foes nor loving friends can hurt you;
If all men count with you, but none too much;
If you can fill the unforgiving minute
With sixty seconds' worth of distance run -
Yours is the Earth and everything that's in it,
And - which is more - you'll be a Man, my son!

Courage

THE BOY WHO DANCED WITH A TANK

Adrian Mitchell (1932-)

It was the same old story
Story of boy meets State
Yes the same old story
Story of boy meets State
The body is created by loving
But a tank's made of fear and hate

Armoured cars and heads in helmets
Rank on rank on rank on rank
The hearts of the soldiers were trembling
But the eyes of the soldiers were blank
And then they saw him swaying -
The boy who danced with a tank

The tank moved left
The boy stepped right
Paused like he was having fun
The tank moved right
The boy stepped left
Smiled at his partner down the barrel of its gun

You remember how we watched him
Dancing like a strong young tree
And we knew that for that moment
He was freer than we'll ever be
A boy danced with a tank in China
Like the flower of liberty

The Feast of Crispian

William Shakespeare (1564-1616)

This day is call'd the feast of Crispian.
He that outlives this day, and comes safe home,
Will stand a-tiptoe when this day is nam'd,
And rouse him at the name of Crispian.
He that shall live this day, and see old age,
Will yearly on the vigil feast his neighbours,
And say 'Tomorrow is Saint Crispian.'
Then will he strip his sleeve and show his scars,
And say 'These wounds I had on Crispian's day.'
Old men forget; yet all shall be forgot,
But he'll remember, with advantages,
What feats he did that day. Then shall our names,
Familiar in his mouth as household words -
Harry the King, Bedford and Exeter,
Warwick and Talbot, Salisbury and Gloucester -
Be in their flowing cups freshly rememb'red.
This story shall the good man teach his son;
And Crispin Crispian shall ne'er go by,
From this day to the ending of the world,
But we in it shall be remembered -
We few, we happy few, we band of brothers;
For he today that sheds his blood with me
Shall be my brother; be he ne'er so vile,
This day shall gentle his condition;
And gentlemen in England now a-bed
Shall think themselves accursed they were not here,
And hold their manhoods cheap whiles any speaks
That fought with us upon Saint Crispin's day.

70   Henry V Act 4 Scene 3

VERGISSMEINNICHT

Keith Douglas (1920-1944)

Three weeks gone and the combatants gone,
returning over the nightmare ground
we found the place again, and found
the soldier sprawling in the sun.

The frowning barrel of his gun
overshadowing. As we came on
that day, he hit my tank with one
like the entry of a demon.

Look. Here in the gunpit spoil
the dishonoured picture of his girl
who has put: *Steffi. Vergissmeinnicht*
in a copybook gothic script.

We see him almost with content
abased, and seeming to have paid
and mocked at by his own equipment
that's hard and good when he's decayed.

But she would weep to see today
how on his skin the swart flies move;
the dust upon the paper eye
and the burst stomach like a cave.

For here the lover and killer are mingled
who had one body and one heart.
And death who had the soldier singled
has done the lover mortal hurt.

Lament for Culloden

Robert Burns (1759-1796)

The lovely lass o' Inverness,
Nae joy nor pleasure can she see;
For e'en and morn she cries, Alas!
And aye the saut tear blins her ee:
Drumossie moor - Drumossie day
A waefu' day it was to me!
For there I lost my father dear,
My father dear, and brethren three.

Their winding-sheet the bluidy clay,
Their graves are growing green to see:
And by them lies the dearest lad
That ever blest a woman's ee
Now wae to thee, thou cruel lord,

A bluidy man I trow thou be,
For mony a heart thou hast made sair
That ne'er did wrang to thine or thee.

ANNE FRANK HUIS

Andrew Motion (1952-)

Even now, after twice her lifetime of grief
and anger in the very place, whoever comes
to climb these narrow stairs, discovers how
the bookcase slides aside, then walks through
shadow into sunlit rooms, can never help

but break her secrecy again. Just listening
is a kind of guilt: the Westerkirk repeats
itself outside, as if all time worked round
towards her fear, and made each stroke
die down on guarded streets. Imagine it -

three years of whispering and loneliness
and plotting, day by day, the Allied line
in Europe with a yellow chalk. What hope
she had for ordinary love and interest
survives her here, displayed above the bed

as pictures of her family; some actors;
fashions chosen by Princess Elizabeth.
And those who stoop to see them find
not only patience missing its reward,
but one enduring wish for chances

like my own: to leave as simply
as I do, and walk at ease
up dusty tree-lined avenues, or watch
a silent barge come clear of bridges
settling their reflections in the blue canal.

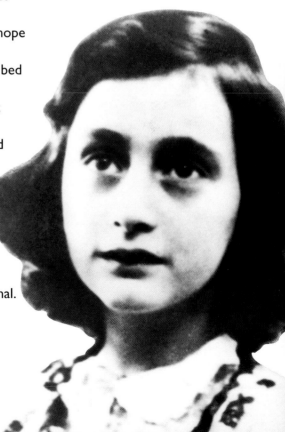

Miners

Wilfred Owen (1893-1918)

There was a whispering in my hearth,
A sigh of the coal,
Grown wistful of a former earth
It might recall.

I listened for a tale of leaves
And smothered ferns;
Frond-forests; and the low, sly lives
Before the fawns.

My fire might show steam-phantoms simmer
From Time's old cauldron,
Before the birds made nests in summer,
Or men had children.

But the coals were murmuring of their mine,
And moans down there
Of boys that slept wry sleep, and men
Writhing for air.

And I saw white bones in the cinder-shard.
Bones without number;
For many hearts with coal are charred
And few remember.

I thought of some who worked dark pits
Of war, and died
Digging the rock where Death reputes
Peace lies indeed.

Comforted years will sit soft-chaired
In rooms of amber;
The years will stretch their hands, well-cheered
By our lives' ember.

The centuries will burn rich loads
With which we groaned,
Whose warmth shall lull their dreaming lids
While songs are crooned.
But they will not dream of us poor lads
Lost in the ground.

LADY IN BLACK

Alun Lewis (1915-1944)

Lady in black,
I knew your son.
Death was our enemy
Death and his gun.

Death had a trench
And he blazed away.
We took that trench
By the end of the day.

Lady in black
Your son was shot.
He was my mate
And he got it hot.

Death's a bastard
Keeps hitting back.
But a war's a war
Lady in black

Birth hurt bad
But you didn't mind.
Well maybe Death
Can be just as kind.

So take it quiet
The same as your son.
Death's only a vicar
Armed with a gun.

And one day Death
Will give it back
And then you can speak to him tidy
Lady in black.

The Drum

John Scott of Amwell (1730-1783)

I hate that drum's discordant sound,
Parading round, and round, and round:
To thoughtless youth it pleasure yields,
And lures from cities and from fields,
To sell their liberty for charms
Of tawdry lace, and glittering arms;
And when Ambition's voice commands,
To march, and fight, and fall, in foreign lands.

I hate that drum's discordant sound,
Parading round, and round, and round:
To me it talks of ravaged plains,
And burning towns, and ruined swains,
And mangled limbs, and dying groans,
And widows' tears, and orphans' moans;
And all that Misery's hand bestows,
To fill the catalogue of human woes.

Legacy

THE TERROR YEARS

Rajko Djuric (1947-)
Translated by Julie Ebin

Our house is Auschwitz,
So big and black. So black and big.
Petals of skull are hidden,
Strewn amidst the tall grass.
Prayers rise up and fall back
Beneath the ashes, beneath the dreams,
Searching for a door, a road out.

House so big. House so black.
Lightless house, hopeless house.

As I arrive at our house
My lips turn blue.
These terror years are my path;
Their names are the way-stations.

Our house is Auschwitz,
So big and black. So black and big.
This is where our tears flow,
Destroying our sight.
This is where they crushed our pleas
For no one to hear.
This is where they turned us to ashes
For the winds to scatter.

Listen, Adam! Listen, Simon!
Eve and Mary, too!
The twenty-five thousand shadows
That watch and follow me:
These terror years are our path;
Their names are the way-stations.

House so big. House so black.
House with no street, house with no address.

Abou Ben Adhem

James Leigh Hunt (1784-1859)

Abou Ben Adhem (may his tribe increase!)
Awoke one night from a deep dream of peace,
And saw, within the moonlight in his room,
Making it rich, and like a lily in bloom,
An angel writing in a book of gold:-
Exceeding peace had made Ben Adhem bold,
And to the presence in the room he said,

   'What writest thou?' - The vision raised its head,
And with a look made of all sweet accord,
Answered, 'The names of those who love the Lord.'
'And is mine one?' said Abou. 'Nay, not so,'
Replied the angel. Abou spoke more low,
But cheerly still; and said, 'I pray thee, then,
Write me as one that loves his fellow men.'

    The angel wrote, and vanished. The next night
It came again with a great wakening light,
And showed the names whom love of God had blest,
And lo! Ben Adhem's name led all the rest.

SUNDAYS

John Lyons (1933-)

Sun always shining on Sundays.
Monday-to-Saturday noise gone.

People different on Sundays:
They look so clean.

Daddy gone to market foreday-mornin.
He come back when sun touching house tops,
he come back with watercress
and tie-up blue crab bubbling spit.

Sunday breakfast is cinnamon hot chocolate,
saltfish bull jhol with zaboca and bakes.

Church. And after church,
Sunday school in organdie frocks,
the colour of white sugarcake,
bright colour ribbon in plaits;
navy blue serge pants,
cream silk shirt and panama hat.

Everybody window open wide, wide
showing off frilly lace curtains.
Everybody radio loud, loud
playing the same hymn.

When we come back home
we change in home-clothes.

No marbles on smooth yard ground.
Tops wide awake in pants pocket:
they not sleep-spinning,
humming on the ground.
Sunday sky kite-free.

No brown girl in the ring
with a tra-la-la-la-la;
no hide-and-seek,
no stick-em-up.
Only nancy stories
and Sunday napping.

Sometimes
the man selling icecream
comes just before we fall asleep.
Grandma likes to chat
and we love the icecream.

Peace

Henry Vaughan (1621-1695)

My soul, there is a country
Far beyond the stars,
Where stands a wingèd sentry
All skilful in the wars:
There above noise and danger
Sweet Peace sits crowned with smiles,
And One born in a manger
Commands the beauteous files.
He is thy gracious friend
And - O my soul, awake! -
Did in pure love descend
To die here for thy sake.
If thou canst get but thither,
There grows the flower of Peace,
The Rose that cannot wither,
Thy fortress, and thy ease.
Leave then thy foolish ranges
For none can thee secure,
But one who never changes,
Thy God, thy life, thy cure.

PAX

D H Lawrence (1885-1930)

All that matters is to be at one with the living God
to be a creature in the house of the God of Life.

Like a cat asleep on a chair
at peace, in peace
and at one with the master of the house, with the mistress,
at home, at home in the house of the living,
sleeping on the hearth, and yawning before the fire.

Sleeping on the hearth of the living world,
yawning at home before the fire of life
feeling the presence of the living God
like a great reassurance
a deep calm in the heart
a presence
as of a master sitting at the board
in his own and greater being,
in the house of life.

Vitaï Lampada

Henry Newbolt (1862-1938)

There's a breathless hush in the Close tonight -
Ten to make and the match to win -
A bumping pitch and a blinding light,
An hour to play and the last man in.
And it's not for the sake of a ribboned coat,
Or the selfish hope of a season's fame,
But his Captain's hand on his shoulder smote -
'Play up! play up! and play the game!'

The sand of the desert is sodden red, -
Red with the wreck of a square that broke; -
The Gatling's jammed and the Colonel dead,
And the regiment blind with dust and smoke.
The river of death has brimmed his banks,
And England's far, and Honour a name,
But the voice of a schoolboy rallies the ranks:
'Play up! play up! and play the game!'

This is the word that year by year,
While in her place the School is set,
Every one of her sons must hear,
And none that hears it dare forget.
This they all with a joyful mind
Bear through life like a torch in flame,
And falling fling to the host behind -
'Play up! play up! and play the game!'

Play on

BY THE WATERS OF LIVERPOOL

Adrian Mitchell (1932-)

So many of her sons drowned in the slime of trenches
So many of her daughters torn apart by poverty
So many of her children died in the darkness
So many of her prisoners slowly crushed in slave-ships
Century after red century the Mersey flowed on by -
By the waters of Liverpool we sat down and wept

      But slaves and the poor know better than anyone
      How to have a real good time
      If you're strong enough to speak
      You're strong enough to sing
      If you can stand up on your feet
      You can stomp out a beat …

So we'd been planning how to celebrate
That great red river of Liverpool
As our team rose to a torrent
That would flood the green of Wembley
We'd been planning how to celebrate
The great red dream of Liverpool
For Dalglish held the Cup in his left fist
And the League in his right -
By the waters of Liverpool we sat down and wept

Our scarves are weeping on the gates of Anfield
And that great singing ground is a palace of whispers
For the joy of the game, the heart of the game,
Yes the great red heart of the great red game
Is broken and all the red flowers of Liverpool -
By the waters of Liverpool we sat down and wept.

April 1989, after Hillsborough

The Pedlar's Caravan

William Brighty Rands (1823-1882)

I wish I lived in a caravan,
With a horse to drive, like the pedlar-man!
Where he comes from nobody knows,
Or where he goes to, but on he goes!

His caravan has windows two,
And a chimney of tin, that the smoke comes through;
He has a wife, with a baby brown,
And they go riding from town to town.

Chairs to mend, and delf to sell!
He clashes the basins like a bell;
Tea-trays, baskets ranged in order,
Plates with the alphabet round the border!

The roads are brown, and the sea is green,
But his house is just like a bathing-machine;
The world is round, and he can ride,
Rumble and splash, to the other side!

With the pedlar-man I should like to roam,
And write a book when I came home;
All the people would read my book,
Just like the Travels of Captain Cook.

THE LONG ROAD

Šaban Iliaz

We took a road into night
unaware of where it might lead.
We left behind a great land
and started our journey of sorrow.

We strayed over many a byway
carrying our heavy loads.
We buried our dead along the way;
in the forests our fathers grew old.

In the midst of the darkest place
we sat ourselves down to rest.
We paused to revive our spirits
and as we sat there, we slept;

No bread we ate nor water drank;
not a crust passed our lips.
When morning came we got up again
and continued along the road.

Travellers

To the Virgins, to Make Much of Time

Robert Herrick (1591-1674)

Gather ye rosebuds while ye may,
Old Time is still a-flying:
And this same flower that smiles to-day
To-morrow will be dying.

The glorious lamp of heaven, the sun,
The higher he's a-getting,
The sooner will his race be run,
And nearer he's to setting.

That age is best which is the first,
When youth and blood are warmer;
But being spent, the worse, and worst
Times still succeed the former.

Then be not coy, but use your time,
And while ye may, go marry:
For having lost but once your prime,
You may for ever tarry.

Time passes

SPRING-CLEANING AT SEVENTY

Edward Lowbury (1913-)

I'm burning up the past, this load of letters;
    Stop now and then to read a page or two.
A few I'll save. What meant so much, those matters
    Of moment, like 'we are pleased to offer you
The post ...' - they bore me now; even messages
    Of friendship read like slogans, hollow stuff;
Nor am I shattered by such passages
    As 'Yes, I like you, but that's not enough'.

A crumpled yellow sheet drops from the pile,
    An unfamiliar hand. I smooth it out
And try to read the faded script:' ... your smile
    Haunts me ... when you are with me I could shout
For joy ... you say "be happy", but I can't -
    You are always in my thoughts, but you're not here';
Signed 'Mary Keats', the writing diffident,
    Shaky, ink-blurred - maybe a tear.

Then suddenly I race back forty years
    To a night ward-round in my hospital
Where Sister Keats has briefed me; next, my ears
    Pick up the distant song of a nightingale
Through the open window, and a crazy whim
    Prompts me to read John Keats to Mary Keats, -
I feel that I'm reciting it to him! -
    While far away that nightingale competes.

But Mary Keats is savouring every line,
    Mirrors in those dark eyes each syllable,
Letting them rest luxuriously on mine.
    'I did not know it was so rich, so full',
She whispers ...
                That was forty years ago:
    Then I believed it was the Ode which gave
Such colour to her cheeks, but I was slow;
    My cheeks burn now. - Her letter I will save.

The Poplar-Field

William Cowper (1731-1800)

The poplars are felled, farewell to the shade
And the whispering sound of the cool colonnade,
The winds play no longer, and sing in the leaves,
Nor Ouse on his bosom their image receives.

Twelve years have elapsed since I last took a view
Of my favourite field and the bank where they grew,
And now in the grass behold they are laid,
And the tree is my seat that once lent me a shade.

The blackbird has fled to another retreat
Where the hazels afford him a screen from the heat,
And the scene where his melody charmed me before,
Resounds with his sweet-flowing ditty no more.

My fugitive years are all hasting away,
And I must ere long lie as lowly as they,
With a turf on my breast, and a stone at my head,
Ere another such grove shall arise in its stead.

'Tis a sight to engage me, if any thing can,
To muse on the perishing pleasures of man,
Though his life be a dream, his enjoyments, I see,
Have a being less durable even than he.

Memories

MY BOX

Gillian Clarke (1937-)

My box is made of golden oak,
my lover's gift to me.
He fitted hinges and a lock
of brass and a bright key.
He made it out of winter nights,
sanded and oiled and planed,
engraved inside the heavy lid
in brass, a golden tree.

In my box are twelve black books
where I have written down
how we have sanded, oiled and planed,
planted a garden, built a wall,
seen jays and goldcrests, rare red kites,
found the wild heartsease, drilled a well,
harvested apples and words and days
and planted a golden tree.

On an open shelf I keep my box.
Its key is in the lock.
I leave it there for you to read,
or them, when we are dead,
how everything is slowly made,
how slowly things made me,
a tree, a lover, words, a box,
books and a golden tree.

Remember

Christina Rossetti (1830-1894)

Remember me when I am gone away,
Gone far away into the silent land;
When you can no more hold me by the hand,
Nor I half turn to go, yet turning stay.
Remember me when no more day by day
You tell me of our future that you planned:
Only remember me, you understand
It will be late to counsel then or pray.

Yet if you should forget me for a while
And afterwards remember, do not grieve:
For if the darkness and corruption leave
A vestige of the thoughts that once I had,
Better by far you should forget and smile
Than that you should remember and be sad.

FINGERS

Ted Hughes (1930-1998)

Who will remember your fingers?
Their winged life? They flew
With the light in your look.
At the piano, stomping out hits from the forties,
They performed an incidental clowning
Routine of their own, deadpan puppets.
You were only concerned to get them to the keys.
But as you talked, as your eyes signalled
The strobes of your elation,
They flared, flicked balletic aerobatics.
I thought of birds in some tropical sexual
Play of display, leaping and somersaulting,
Doing strange things in the air, and dropping to the dust.
Those dancers of your excess!
With such deft, practical touches - so accurate.
Thinking their own thoughts caressed like lightning
The lipstick into your mouth corners.

Trim conductors of your expertise,
Cavorting at your typewriter,
Possessed by infant spirit, puckish,
Who, whatever they did, danced or mimed it
In a weightless largesse of espressivo.

I remember your fingers. And your daughter's
Fingers remember your fingers
In everything they do.
Her fingers obey and honour your fingers,
The Lares and Penates of our house.

Author Index

W.H.Auden
Twelve Songs IX — 21
George Barker
To My Mother — 9
Thomas Lovell Bedoes
Dream-Pedlary — 26
William Blake
London — 58
The Little Black Boy — 64
The School Boy — 60
The Tyger — 46
Robert Burns
Robert Bruce's March
to Bannockburn — 66
Lament for Culloden — 72
John Clare
Hares at Play — 48
Gillian Clarke
My Box — 89
Susan Coolidge
Measles in the Ark — 8
William Cowper
The Poplar-Field — 88
E.E.Cummings
Spring is Like a Perhaps Hand — 41
Emily Dickinson
There's Been A Death — 56
Rajko Djurić
The Terror Years — 77
John Donne
Death be not Proud — 22
Keith Douglas
Vergissmeinnicht — 71
Douglas Dunn
Second Opinion — 17
U.A.Fanthorpe
Half-Term — 61
Andrew Fusek Peters
Scattering the Ashes — 22-23
Zulfikar Ghose
Conspiracy of the Clouds — 44 – 45

Philip Gross
The Twenty-Sixers — 54 – 55
Thomas Hardy
The Wedding Morning — 14
Seamus Heaney
A Call — 25
Field of Vision — 67
Widgeon — 33
Robert Herrick
To The Virgins, to Make Much of Time — 86
Gerard Manly Hopkins
The Windhover — 32
Thomas Hood
No! — 38
Ted Hughes
Fingers — 91
Mooses — 49
James Leigh Hunt
Abou Ben Adhem — 78
Jackie Kay
Waves — 35
John Keats
La Belle Dame Sans Merci — 28 – 29
To Autumn — 40 - 41
On First Looking Into — 52
Chapman's Homer
Savan Iliaz
The Long Road — 85
Rudyard Kipling
If — 68
DH Lawrence
Pax — 81
Alun Lewis
Lady in Black — 75
Edward Lowbury
Chickweed — 37
Winter — 39
Spring-Cleaning at Seventy — 87
John Lyons
Sundays — 79

Christopher Marlowe
The Passionate Shepherd to His Love 12

John Milton
On His Blindness 16

Adrian Mitchell
By the Waters of Liverpool 83
The Boy Who Danced With A Tank 69
The Perils of Reading Fiction 51

John Mole
A Tall Story 63

Andrew Motion
Anne Frank Huis 73

Thomas Nashe
In Time of Pestilence 20

Henry Newbolt
Vitaï Lampada 82

Gareth Owen
Moggy in the City 47
Street Boy 59

Wilfrid Owen
Miners 74

Dorothy Parker
One Perfect Rose 11

Sylvia Plath
Morning Song 7

Alexander Pope
A Little Learning 50

William Brighty Rands
The Pedlar's Caravan 8

Christina Rossetti
By the Sea 34
Remember 90

George Santayana
With You a Part of Me Hath Passed Away 2

John Scott of Amwell
The Drum 76

Sir Walter Scott
The Nativity Chant 61

William Shakespeare
My Mistress' Eyes 10
The Feast Of Crispian 70

Stevie Smith
Fairy Story 31

Spiritual
Steal Away to Jesus 18

Robert Louis Stevenson
Windy Nights 62

Alfred, Lord Tennyson
Crossing the Bar 24

Henry Vaughan
Peace 80

Judith Viorst
A Visit From My Mother-In-Law 15

Dorothy Wordsworth
Address to a Child 42 - 43
During a Boisterous Winter Evening

William Wordsworth
Daffodils 36

W.B. Yeats
He Wishes for the Cloths of Heaven 27
When You Are Old 13

Andrew Young
Winter 39

Benjamin Zephaniah
Neighbours 57
White Comedy 65

Acknowledgements

WHAuden: 'Twelve Songs IX', from *Collected Poems*. By permission of Faber and Faber.
George Barker: 'To My Mother', from *Collected Poems*. By permission of Faber and Faber.
Gillian Clarke: 'My Box', from *Letting in the Rumour*. By permission of Carcanet Press.
E.E. Cummings: 'Spring is like a perhaps hand' is reprinted from COMPLETE POEMS 1904-1962, by E.E.Cummings, edited by George J. Firmage, by permission of W.W. Norton & Company. Copyright © 1991 by the Trustees for the E.E Cummings Trust and George James Firmage.
Rajko Djuric: 'The Terror Years', from *The Roads of the Roma*: a PEN anthology of Gipsy writers; edited by Ian Hancock, Siobhan Dowd and Rajko Djuric, University of Hertfordshire Press, 1998. By permission of the University of Hertfordshire Press.
Keith Douglas: 'Vergessmeinicht', from *Collected Poems*. By permission of Faber and Faber.
Douglas Dunn: 'Second Opinion', from *Elegies*. By permission of Faber and Faber.
UA Fanthorpe: 'Half term', Copyright UA Fanthorpe from *Standing To*. (1982 reproduced by permission of Peterloo Poets.)
Andrew Fusek Peters: 'Scattering the Ashes', first published in *May the Angels Be With Us, Poems of Life, Love, AIDS & Death*, by Shropshire Education Publications, 1994. By permission of Andrew Fusek-Peters.
Philip Gross: 'The Twenty Sixers', from *Manifold Manor*. By permission of Faber and Faber.
Seamus Heaney: 'A Call', 'Widgeon' and 'Field of Vision', all from OPENED GROUND: SELECTED POEMS 1966-1996 . Copyright © 1998 by Seamus Heaney. reprinted by permission of Faber and Faber (UK), and Farrar, Strauss and Giroux , LLC (US).
Ted Hughes: 'Mooses', from *Collected Animal Poems*. By permission of Faber and Faber. 'Fingers', from *Birthday Letters*. By permission of Faber and Faber Limited.
Paul Hyland: 'Best Bone', from *The Stubborn Forest*, published by Bloodaxe. By permission of David Higham Associates.
Saban Iliaz: 'The Long Road', from *The Roads of the Roma*: a PEN anthology of Gipsy writers; edited by Ian Hancock, Siobhan Dowd and Rajko Djuric, University of Hertfordshire Press, 1998. By permission of the University of Hertfordshire Press
Jackie Kay: 'Waves'. This poem first appeared in *Two's Company*. Copyright © Jackie Kay.
Rudyard Kipling; 'If''. Reprinted by permission of A.P.Watt Ltd, on behalf of The National Trust for Places of Historic Interest of Natural Beauty.
DH Lawrence: 'Pax'. First published by Heinemann, (Viking in US). Published by arrangement with the estate of DH Lawrence.
Alun Lewis: 'Lady in Black' by Alun Lewis from *Collected Poems*, published by Seren Books, 1994. By permission of Alun Lewis.

Edward Lowbury: 'Chickweed' from *Mystic Bridge*, published by Hippopotamus Press, 1997. 'Spring Cleaning at Seventy', from *Selected and New Poems 1939 – 1989*, published by Hippopotamus Press, 1990. By kind permission of Edward Lowbury.
John Lyons: 'Sundays', from *Behind The Carnival*, by John Lyons, published by Smith/Doorstop Books, 1994. By permission of John Lyons.
Adrian Mitchell: 'The Perils of Reading Fiction', 'By the Waters of Liverpool' and 'The Boy Who Danced with a Tank', © Adrian Mitchell, from *Blue Coffee*, published by Bloodaxe 1996. Reprinted by permission of PFD on behalf of Adrian Mitchell.
John Mole: 'A Tall Story', from *The Dummy's Dilemma*, published by Hodder's Children's Books 1999. By permission of John Mole.
Andrew Motion: 'Anne Frank Huis', from *Selected Poems*, published by Penguin. By permission of Peters, Fraser and Dunlop.
Gareth Owen: 'Street Boy' and 'Moggy in the City', from *Collected Poems for Children*, published by Macmillan Books. Copyright © Gareth Owen 2000. Reproduced by permission of the author c/o Rogers, Coleridge & White Ltd., 20 Powis Mews, London W11 1JN.
Dorothy Parker: 'One Perfect Rose', from *The Collected Dorothy Parker*. By permission of Gerald Duckworth & Co. Ltd.
Sylvia Plath: 'Morning Song', from *Collected Poems*. By permission of Faber and Faber Limited.
George Santayana: 'With You a Part of Me Hath Passed Away', from *The Complete Poems of Santayana*, published by Associated University Presses.
Judith Viorst: 'A Visit from My Mother-in-Law', reprinted from *It's Hard to be Hip Over Thirty and Other Tragedies of Married Life*, by Judith Viorst (Persephone Books, London EC1V 0DS tel 020 7253 5454)
WB Yeats: 'He Wishes for the Cloths of Heaven' and 'When You Are Old'. By permission of Macmillan.
Andrew Young: 'Winter', from *Selected Poems*. By permission of Carcanet Press.
Benjamin Zephaniah: 'Neighbours' and 'White Comedy', from *Propa Propaganda*, published by Bloodaxe Books, 1996. By permission of Bloodaxe Books.

Every effort has been made to trace the copyright holders but in some cases this has not proved possible. The publisher will be happy to rectify any such errors or omissions in future reprints and or new editions.